**Praise for *Don't You Dare Get Married
Until You Read This!***

"Helps couples better understand the potential land mines in
their relationship."
—Jeff Zaslow, *Chicago Sun-Times*

"A workbook that promises the marriage-minded a picture of
how compatible they really are."
—Kay Harvey, *St. Paul Pioneer Press*

"Heed the warning, Don't You Dare Get Married Until You
Read This!"
—Mark Wolf, *Denver Rocky Mountain News*

"This book leaves no issue untouched, and it's ideal for
couples who may be leery of premarital counseling or
unable to afford it."
—Doug Carrol, *Arizona Republic*

"Look into those frightening areas of your relationship, and
you'll see Donaldson's book staring right back at you."
—Rob McDonald, *Fort Wayne News-Sentinel*

"A provocative primer for couples contemplating marriage."
—Beth Cooney, *Stamford* (Connecticut) *Advocate*

"Real essential and confronting. As an engaged man I found that this book leaves no stone unturned, no questions unasked. A must-have for all engaged couples."
—Dale Dorning (Sydney, Australia)

"[This book] makes you stop! . . . and *think*. Many of the questions that should be discussed beforehand are too often 'covered up' because we are too busy putting our best foot forward, instead of being honest and realistic about our life. It helped me see how much time and care are needed when seeking a companion."
—Trudie Fullmer (Salt Lake City, Utah)

"If you really, truly want to get to know the person you want to marry someday, try this book and be honest; knowing this information up-front will help you decide if marriage is right and your partner is the right one for you. It saves a lot of guesswork and may save a lot of heartache later on."
—Paul Coombs (Ogden, Utah)

"If you are planning a marriage, not a wedding, then this would be a great book for you. It has given me a lot of different views on marriage and has helped me be better prepared for the issues that *do* come up in marriage."
—Pattie Graven (Ogden, Utah)

"[This book] is especially good for those who get engaged after dating a short time. . . . It makes you think about things in your relationship and helps you get to know yourself and your companion better."
—Anita Longhurst (West Jordan, Utah)

DON'T YOU DARE GET MARRIED

UNTIL YOU READ THIS!

DON'T YOU DARE GET MARRIED UNTIL YOU READ THIS!

The book of questions for couples

COREY DONALDSON

 THREE RIVERS PRESS • NEW YORK

Published by Three Rivers Press, New York, New York.
Member of the Crown Publishing Group.

Random House, Inc. New York, Toronto, London, Sydney, Auckland
www.randomhouse.com

THREE RIVERS PRESS is a registered trademark and the
Three Rivers Press colophon is a trademark of Random House, Inc.

Originally published by Sentinel Publishing in 2000.

Printed in the United States of America

Design by Susan Maksuta

Library of Congress Cataloging-in-Publication Data
Donaldson, Corey.
Don't you dare get married until you read this : the book of questions for
couples/by Corey Donaldson.
1. Marriage—Handbooks, manuals, etc.   I. Title.
HQ734.D695 2001
306.81—dc21   00–066326

ISBN 0-609-80783-8 (pbk.)

10 9 8 7 6 5 4 3 2 1

Revised and Updated Edition

To Phaidra,
my beautiful wife, who motivates me
to be the "right one"

 **CONTENTS**

CONTENTS

DON'T YOU DARE GET MARRIED

UNTIL YOU READ THIS!

WHY IS THIS BOOK NECESSARY AND WHAT RESEARCH IS BEHIND IT?

There is very little optimism left in this world when it comes to the institution of marriage.

The U.S. Census Bureau reports the following statistics:

- Since 1970 there has been a decline of more than one-third in the annual number of marriages per one thousand women.
- People are marrying later: The average age at first marriage today is twenty-five for women, twenty-seven for men, whereas twenty years ago, it was twenty-two for women and twenty-four for men.

- The percentage of adults in the population at any one time who are married has also diminished. However, the number of unmarried cohabitating couples continues to increase (865 percent since 1960).

- The percentage of adults who are presently divorced has quadrupled since 1960.

- The number of intact married couples who rate their marriage as "very happy" has decreased. (In 1973, 67.4 percent said their marriages were "very happy." That percentage decreased to 61.9 percent in 1996.) It has been estimated that after ten years only 25 percent of first marriages are successful (i.e., intact and reportedly happy).

- The percentage of children in single-parent families has risen from 9 percent in 1960 to 28 percent in 1998. Thirty-five percent of children now live apart from their biological fathers.

- Out of 41.6 million men, 15.8 million are unmarried. Of those, 11.9 million have never married, 3.8 million are divorced, and 124,000 are widowed.

- Out of 42.1 million women, 13.7 million are single. Of those, 8.6 million never married, 4.7 million are divorced, and 394,000 are widowed.

The reason this book is necessary should be abundantly clear without reference to any statistics or reports. In today's society, divorce is playing a part in *everyone's* life. It has become the solution to a problem that could have been resolved long before. Divorce is not (in most cases) the result of a bad marriage; it is the punishment for not preparing before the marriage took place.

It seems that we as human beings prefer to repeat our own mistakes over and over again regardless of the clear lessons laid out before us. Otto von Bismarck said, "The fool learns from his own mistakes. I would rather learn from the mistakes of others." Certainly there are many people who are plagued with mistakes of their own from which even they do not learn. I propose that we become more observant of the lessons in life that must be learned. Look at other people and vow not to repeat their stupidity, or emulate their fine example as the case may be.

While compiling this book, I have made every effort to observe the lessons taught by the experiences of others. From the point at which I began the first version of this book until now, I have interviewed more than fifteen hundred people. I have made a genuine effort to get as wide a cross section of people as possible. I have interviewed and spoken with divorcées, singles, teenagers, married people, engaged couples, lawyers, social workers, TV reporters, and radio personalities. The question I asked these people most was, "If you could only ask one question of your partner before you got married, what would it be?" Their answers are in this book. Obviously I do not have anywhere near fifteen hundred questions in this book because many gave the same answer or something similar to it.

This book also benefits from a significant input from journalists such as Jeff Zaslow of the *Chicago Sun-Times*. Jeff asked his readers to send in questions they thought should be considered before a marriage takes place. Hundreds of questions were sent in, but I already had most of them. Nevertheless, this book includes up to forty innovative and intriguing questions from Jeff's readers. Thank you to Jeff and his loyal following!

It will become clear very quickly that the number of sex questions far outweighs any of the others. This is not because I have some abnormal preoccupation with sex, nor do I want to be your aid in exploring your sordid fantasies as far as they relate only to yourself. Rather, my purpose is to help you to understand your sexual relationship with your partner and your own unique sexual dimensions and limitations. It will be of interest to you to know that the overwhelming majority of the sex questions came from letters written by readers of the self-published version of this book, which I released in 1998. Many letters talked about how this book injected some wisdom into their minds and helped them prepare for making such a big decision, but they also discussed the shortfall of sex questions. Sex is a major problem in many marriages, and my readers felt the need for a more in-depth exploration of the sexual relationship and therefore offered questions that should be included in the book.

As you read the questions in this book, remember that they are here because of other people's mistakes and triumphs in life, or perhaps because of the lessons they have learned from others. Either way you look at it, please realize that preparing for marriage matters. *Marriage matters because happiness matters. This is one of those moments in life where your perspective, attitude, and focus really count. You do not get a second chance to get it right the first time.*

A COURTSHIP FROM ACROSS THE WORLD

I have no reservation in declaring that the time from January to October of 1996 was one of the most significant stages in my life. This was the time of my engagement to Phaidra Benincosa. This time period was especially important because I was preparing for one of the most critical decisions of my life: marriage.

After writing back and forth for a number of years between Salt Lake City, Utah, and Melbourne, Australia, Phaidra and I finally met in December 1995. At the beginning of January, we announced our desire to spend the rest of our lives together. We were engaged to be married.

The decision was one made on faith because so many problems and challenges confronted us. My roots were in Australia, and Phaidra's were in Utah. She was studying at school; I had work. We both had friends and family who meant everything to us. What could we do? Phaidra returned to Salt Lake City three days after our engagement with no wedding date set. Any goals we had together seemed unrealistic and obscure. We had no idea how we were going to marry and where to do it. We knew only that we wanted to.

The next few months provided opportunity for more growth than either of us had ever experienced. First came feelings of doubt since we were now apart and without each other's support. Questions arose in our minds. Did we really know each other? We had only seen each other in a vacation atmosphere. Anyone can fall in love on vacation. We didn't know what the other person was like in a day-to-day normal life. Would our different cultures cause problems? In which country would we live and raise our children? How could either of us afford to leave his or her native country and then get married? Would homesickness prevent the peaceful longevity of the relationship? Furthermore, how would each family feel about losing a son or daughter to the other?

Unanswered questions were not the only frustrations we experienced during these first few months. Although doubts and difficulties remained, we missed each other intensely. We felt a genuine kinship and love for each other, feelings that we knew needed further development. The best medium available to assist in developing our relationship was letter writing, which we agreed to do once a week. We acknowledged the need to get to know each other more intimately, spend more quality time together, and ask each other questions that revealed more about ourselves.

The value of asking questions became immediately apparent because it helped us identify with each other and further develop our love by accepting the idiosyncrasies of our personalities. How else could I find out that whenever Phaidra eats fries, she stirs up a mixture of mayonnaise and ketchup, usually on hamburger wrapping paper? How else could I learn that she likes twelve pillows on the bed instead of just two, or that I have to match my clothes; that she likes to be romanced on days when I don't feel like it, that I have to remember birthdays and anniversaries and be on call to administer foot rubs at her request? How else could I discover that she dislikes my colored clothing being washed with her whites, that the bathroom has to be cleaned every week, or that dishes have to be washed immediately after dinner (even if *Monday Night Football* is on)?

Phaidra and I understood that the decision to marry should not be taken lightly. The knowledge we gained, the information we received, and the emotions we shared by writing letters proved very worthwhile. However, although letter writing had its merits, it also had obvious limitations.

At the end of March, it was decided that I would leave Melbourne and join Phaidra in Salt Lake City. The decision was made only a week before I left. This was the longest week of my life. So many thoughts were running through my head. I could not wait to see Phaidra. I spent every moment thinking about my reunion with her at the airport. I had an image in my mind that I would see her as I was coming off the plane; romantic music would echo in the background as we bounded toward each other, in slow motion of course, like the movies. Our embrace would be cut short only by a yearning for that first kiss, making up for three long, lost months.

So much for dreams and images. As it turned out, I was deliberately the last one off the plane. Somehow the anticipation, nervousness, and excitement had a restraining effect on me. When I finally saw Phaidra, there was no romantic prelude music, and she was conversing with some stranger. Once our eyes met, there was definitely no slow motion. We embraced each other as if there were no tomorrow, basking in the exquisite joy of being in each other's arms.

Finally we were in an environment where, because we had decided to make our home in Utah, we could begin to plan our marriage in a practical manner. We knew that planning our lives beyond marriage was important, that planning the wedding itself was important. Nevertheless, nothing took priority over making efforts to know each other in day-to-day life. Now we could see each other under stress. Now we could see each other in different situations. It was so important to experience all of these conditions if we were to know each other. In addition, we never stopped asking questions, talking to each other, and thoroughly enjoying each other's company. Yes, there was a time to just have fun, talking, joking and being jovial, but the moments to be serious were also essential.

As time passed, the questions we asked became more probing. Occasionally they even led to confrontation. However, rather than resulting in painful arguments, these questions led to a mutual respect of each other's feelings. At times it was difficult to deal with the answers some of the questions demanded. The irritation and frustration seemed so unnecessary when we were going through it. Why should we deal with issues that might not even arise during our marriage? Phaidra and I reasoned that such emotions were better to experience before marriage, not after, but we decided to keep tension to a minimum by concentrating on the most predictable issues. The central focus of our questions to each other during our engagement was determining our compatibility, deciding whether we were even suited for marriage in the first place. To some extent, the decision to marry a person is more important than what happens afterward.

Our love and consideration for each other grew tremendously. In the beginning, we felt that marriage should not take place until we knew each other so well that it was as if we were already married. In October of 1996, we were finally prepared. We knew each other and what we should and should not expect.

Throughout our engagement, through thick and thin, we felt the kinship of our souls. What a joy it was to have peace of mind and soul on our wedding day. I knew Phaidra and I were to be one. It was the happiest day of my life.

WHY YOU SHOULD ASK QUESTIONS BEFORE YOU GET MARRIED

He who asks the questions cannot avoid the answer.

CAMEROON PROVERB

Phaidra and I still have much to learn; indeed, learning from each other will never cease. It surprises me to see how many marriages among young couples break up. I wonder if it is rare for couples really to know each other before they are married. I have noticed that there are couples who prepare very poorly for a decision that will have tremendous impact on their lives. Each couple has its own reasons for breaking up. Some divorces cannot be helped. Some scenarios that couples face in marriage cannot be predicted, so they cannot be prepared for. On the other hand, I have known couples to confess that they knew their marriages would not last even before they were married, and yet they got married anyway. Is it any wonder we have so many personal and social problems when we cannot even get our relationships right from the beginning?

If engaged couples were more assertive in asking relevant questions of each other, they could prepare more thoroughly for what the future holds. I agree with the wise words of author Anthony Robbins when he said, "Relationships flourish when people ask the right questions about where potential conflict exists and how to support each other instead of tearing each other down."

Do we ever ask ourselves if we really know the person we are going to marry? Many claim they do, yet once the marriage occurs, that knowledge proves to be ignorance that evolves into a lifetime of despair. Such ignorance needs to be overcome by asking questions that extract attitudes and opinions. Without taking this initiative, how can we

- expect to know the person we want a commitment with?

- realize the significance of knowing a person we want to spend our lives with?
- give careful thought to the questions we must ask to obtain the information we need to make a decision that has lifelong consequences?

To boast of *knowing* an individual, time must be spent together having fun, sharing intelligent conversation, meeting family and friends, participating in spiritual and emotional moments, surviving tough times, and asking the right questions. Often, asking the right questions is not recognized as a significant element in getting to know the person you are going to marry. Hence, soon after their marriages, couples who fail to ask the necessary questions are confronted with disillusionment, surprise, anxiety, and discontent, which may lead to a quick breakup. If only people would spend more time getting to know the person they want to marry than they do buying a house, car, or television, or thinking about household furniture and decorations, or even the clothes they wear for a special occasion. Unfortunately, it seems that in modern society, purchasing these items consumes more time, energy, and planning than preparing for a marriage.

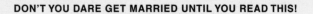

The difference between what you know and what you do not know about your partner lies in the questions you ask. A decision to marry a person is based on only the information you have. Would your decision to marry stand if you had more information about your partner than you currently have? Maybe you still would or perhaps you wouldn't. The fact remains that the difference between what you know and what you don't know will only become apparent by asking the right questions.

Imagine the plight of a child who was forbidden to ask questions. How would this child ever increase in knowledge? What would it be like if police officers could never ask questions of alleged criminals? How could they ever determine who is a criminal and who isn't, let alone solve any crimes? How would a journalist write an article without the ability to ask questions? What would an ambulance officer do if forbidden to ask questions of an accident victim with internal injuries? Are you getting the idea? The point is that a significant proportion of the information we gather in our lives comes through the questions we ask. Therefore, since marriage is arguably the most important decision we will make in our lives, it stands to reason that we must approach it with the right questions.

The interviews I have conducted with well over fifteen hundred people show overwhelmingly that *the majority of divorce-causing problems exist before the wedding takes place.* If couples knew beforehand that they would get divorced and the reasons causing it, would they still get married? I hope not! Well, this knowledge is available by asking the right questions before the knot is tied. The answers to the questions you ask will give you a glimpse into the future and show you what marriage to a certain person will be like.

A certain distinction needs to be made about your focus when asking questions. When trying to determine if you are marrying the right person, your focus needs to be long term, not short term. You must not think that your relationship looks pretty good until the honeymoon is over, and then hope for the best. This is only a good way to think if you want a quick divorce and a rapid increase of misery in your life. If your goals are somewhat different, you must plan for the future, not just allow it to happen. Use vision when asking questions of your partner; ask yourself if you can realistically live with this person with the answers you are hearing. Of course, you won't love everything about your partner, but you cannot expect to live with things you can't or won't be able to tolerate.

In our lives, we spend more time thinking about those things that matter to us than the less important ones. This being the case, it should follow that we invest more time preparing for and maintaining our marriage than anything else because it should be our highest priority. If we do not dedicate a great deal of time to the person we are planning to marry, then we have no business making the commitment. We need to be mature enough to recognize that marriage has a greater impact on our lives than anything else and acknowledge its importance by asking the right questions the right way.

Many offer excuses for not asking their prospective partner probing questions. They claim they don't want to interrogate the other person or disrupt "lovey-dovey" feelings. These questions should not create hard feelings. Rather they should stimulate a feeling of mutual love and concern. Finding excuses for not asking relevant questions avoids the reality that must be confronted after the marriage. The person who avoids learning as much as possible about the other person before marriage risks discovering something distasteful later. Such a discovery can cause misery that might have been avoided by a responsible approach. *To those who say that asking questions is unromantic, uncomfortable, or awkward, I say, so is a divorce!*

The only fair expectation you can have about your partner as you read through this book is that you will discover weaknesses. As you start identifying with your partner, you will have disagreements, discover areas for improvement, and uncover issues your partner may want to talk about in the future or not at all. Whatever the case, you must be diplomatic about respecting the feelings of your partner and never demand an answer when one is not forthcoming. It is not a sin to disagree, have different points of view, or even postpone commenting on a particular issue. You will not love everything about your partner. If you think otherwise, then you do not know your partner well enough. It is important to acknowledge that it is okay to love someone you feel has weaknesses. After all, your partner should feel the same way.

To say there is a correct or incorrect way of asking these questions presumes that I know the dynamics of every personality and relationship, and I don't. However, I do have some suggestions that may be of value. Often these questions can be part of a conversation at home in the TV room, over the table at a restaurant, or out on a picnic. Some couples may find only a few questions relevant and may agree to discuss just them. Individuals may have particular concerns and may need to approach their partner more formally to address some issues. Some people may even want to memorize pertinent questions and raise them randomly at an appropriate time. You may choose a serious or a fun approach. I suggest a combination of both.

Please keep in mind that the person asking the questions receives the most information. However, there are moments when the person asking the questions is providing the most information by the way he or she does it. Never place limitations on the conditions in which one can learn from a partner.

Carefully considering the questions in this book will definitely help you and your prospective partner. The results of the questions will be readily apparent. Please pose each question to your partner and have him or her ask you in return. I guarantee that your mind will be stretched to its limits, and you will discover unknown new dimensions in your partner.

The following is an excerpt from a letter I wrote to Phaidra after we announced our engagement. Phaidra was in Utah, and I was in a painful abyss without her, which at this time was Sydney, Australia.

A brief glimpse at the past few letters we have written indicate a new level of awareness, the awareness that if we were together, we would be getting to know each other a lot better. However, we aren't together, so letters must be the tools we use. The tools we use in letters are questions: questions to find out what makes us tick, sometimes loaded questions like yours, for instance. You asked if I would swim naked at the beach, but what you were really asking is do I feel comfortable with my body. Am I right or wrong? Anyway, here is a new list of questions for you to get excited about:

1. *Are you comfortable with your (sexy) body?*
2. *Why do you think I am such a fashion bug? (sarcasm)*
3. *How have you dealt with conflict in your family?*
4. *How will you know when you are ready to marry?*

5. *What sort of relationship should we have before we get married?*

6. *Would you want to spend the rest of your life with me if I never changed from the way I am now?*

7. *Do you believe that it is okay to talk about your private life with anyone who will listen?*

8. *What issues do you believe should remain between you and your partner only?*

9. *What feelings are hard for you to talk about?*

10. *Are there issues that you would confide to your friends but not your lover? (That's me, by the way.)*

11. *What have you learned from past relationships?*

12. *If I asked your previous partners to list their biggest complaints about you, what would they say?*

13. *When you are in a bad mood, how should I deal with it?*

14. *In a marriage, do you believe that each partner has the responsibility to fulfill his or her own needs or that each person fills the needs of the other?*

● 15. If you ever do something that bothers me, what is the best way for me to bring it to your attention without causing conflict?

So there it is. These questions should keep you busy for a while. It will be hard enough thinking about them, let alone giving answers. I'm sure I will be responding to your questions soon enough. I can't wait to analyze.

I love you, my sweetness. Be good, be awesome, be my lover, and I'll be your back rubber.

I love you,

Corey

SEX,
ROMANCE,
AND
LOVE

One thing I wish I had known before our honeymoon is that it takes practice to get it right and feel comfortable. On my honeymoon I had imagined a night full of intimacy like you see on television. I thought my wife and I would love it and that it would be lots of fun. However, things did not turn out as expected. After trying intercourse several times, we failed. In fact, for the next two weeks we tried every night to have intercourse, but without success. We have been married for three months now, and we are just beginning to have sex without my wife feeling so much pain. I wish I would have known before I got married that this might happen.

COMMENT FROM A NEW HUSBAND FROM
BETWEEN HUSBAND AND WIFE

1. If we eliminated physical attraction from our relationship, what would be left?

2. Do you think it could be an advantage to have no other sexual experience to compare your wife or husband against? In other words, can virginity be something positive to bring to a marriage?

3. What color would you use to describe your sexual prowess?

4. What one word would you use to describe your sexual personality? Why?

5. What type of music describes the way you make love? Why?

6. What animal would you use to describe your sexual personality? Why?

7. What car best fits your sexual personality? Why?

8. What famous person do you think has your sexual personality? Why?

9. Are you sexually inhibited?

10. What will you do if the passion between us dies and you meet someone who rekindles that passion?

11. If you ranked yourself as a lover, using a scale of one (the worst) to ten (the best), where would you be? What would it take to get you to a ten?

12. What is the best way for me to show that I love you?

13. If I put on weight, will it affect our sexual relationship? How?

14. How often have you invented a headache or some other ailment to avoid having sex?

15. When we go on vacation, do you see it as an opportunity for more lovemaking?

16. If you could only have sex one more time in your life, where and how would you do it?

People never seem to settle into relationships with each other as flesh and blood human beings until they are out of the romantic love stage, until they love each other instead of being "in love."

ROBERT A. JOHNSON,
THE PSYCHOLOGY OF ROMANTIC LOVE

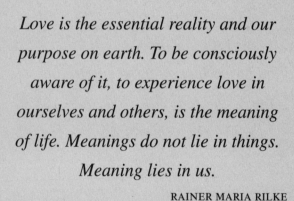

Love is the essential reality and our purpose on earth. To be consciously aware of it, to experience love in ourselves and others, is the meaning of life. Meanings do not lie in things. Meaning lies in us.

RAINER MARIA RILKE

17. How would it affect you if you never had sex again?

18. Are you more interested in making love or having sex? Do you understand the difference?

19. Where does sex rank in life's priorities for you?

20. Do you think sex is overrated?

21. How often do you think about sex?

22. Do you think you are preoccupied with sex?

23. What makes you feel sexy?

24. Do you know what the best way to arouse me is?

25. If female, what's your favorite part of the male body? If male, what's your favorite part of the female body? What's your favorite part of your own body?

26. When we begin to make love, do you prefer to be undressed by me or already be completely naked?

*All men hate to hear, "We need to talk about our relationship." These seven words strike fear in the heart of even General Schwarzkopf.

*Women take clothing much more seriously than men. I've never seen a man walk into a party and say, "Oh my, I'm so embarrassed; get me out of here. There's another man wearing a black tuxedo."

*If you want to get rid of a man without hurting his masculinity, just say, "I love you . . . I want to marry you . . . I want to have your children."

*Men forget everything; women remember everything. That's why men need instant replays. They have already forgotten what happened.

*Women never have anything to wear. Don't question the racks of clothes in their closet. You "just don't understand."

*Women always go to public restrooms in groups. It gives them a chance to gossip.

*Young son: Is it true, Dad? I heard that in some parts of Africa, a man doesn't know his wife until he marries her.

Dad: That happens in every country, son.

SOURCES UNKNOWN

27. Have you ever paid for sex?

28. Could you make love to me if I had bad breath?

29. Describe your dream date.

30. How do you like to be romanced?

31. Would it bother you if I expected you to initiate affection all the time?

32. How do you feel about being affectionate in public?

33. In what ways am I romantic or not romantic? Do you feel you are in love with me the way I am, or with my potential?

34. Are you comfortable talking about sex? Why or why not?

35. Do you believe that we should talk about sex to enhance the experience for each of us?

36. Would you be comfortable if we talked about sex in terms of what we each liked or disliked?

God designed sex to be a relationship that is full of respect and mutual consent. It should be a joyful experience that has an element of pure fun, full of gentle touching, and extended foreplay.

ELIZABETH BAKER

37. Do you believe that sex is spoiled if it is talked about or that it should just come instinctively?

38. Would you consider making love early in the morning?

39. How long should lovemaking last?

40. Are you comfortable making love in the same position all the time or do you prefer change? How frequent should the changes be?

41. Who should decide what position to use when we make love?

42. If premature ejaculation is a problem, how can we deal with it?

43. Do you like sex to be fast or slow?

44. Are there times when you prefer quick sex? When are they?

45. If you didn't have an orgasm, do you say so or fake it?

For a man, romantic experiences with his wife are warm and enjoyable and memorable—but not necessary. For a woman, they are her lifeblood.

DR. JAMES DOBSON

DON'T YOU DARE GET MARRIED UNTIL YOU READ THIS!

46. Do you approve or disapprove of learning different sex techniques from books?

47. Are you embarrassed by talking about sexual issues?

48. Is it important for you to know that I am a virgin? Why or why not?

49. Are you more concerned with being loved or loving? What is the difference?

50. What do I do that causes you to question my love for you?

51. If you are waiting until getting married before you have sex, what is an appropriate way to prepare for your wedding night?

52. What behavior is inappropriate for those who intend to practice sexual abstinence before marriage?

53. What makes you think you are or are not an affectionate person?

A major characteristic of couples who have a happy sex life is that they see lovemaking as an expression of intimacy, but they don't take any differences in their needs or desires personally.

JOHN GOTTMAN, PH.D.,
THE SEVEN PRINCIPLES
OF MAKING MARRIAGE WORK

Those who allow the marriage ceremony to terminate the days of courtship are making a well-nigh fatal mistake. Evidences and tokens of your love and daily proof of your unselfishness toward her [your wife] and your family will make love's flame burn more brightly with the years. Do you girls suppose that the same attention to personal details is less important after marriage? Surely the same qualities and traits in you that first attracted him are just as important in married life in keeping the flame of his affection and romantic desire.

HAROLD LEE

54. When do you believe you were most romantic with me? Was it an occasion that you totally initiated?

55. What makes you feel good about being with me?

56. How do you feel about making love outdoors?

57. What turns you off sexually?

58. If you are doing something sexually that really bothers me, how can I make you aware of it without upsetting you?

59. Do you focus more on pleasing me or yourself when we have sex? Is this good or bad? Why?

60. On a scale from one to ten (with ten as the highest), how would you grade your skills in the bedroom?

61. What do you want to change about my sexual performance?

62. What do I do that gives you the most sexual pleasure?

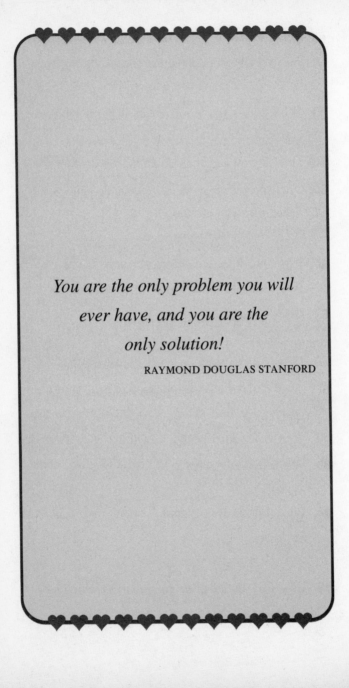

You are the only problem you will ever have, and you are the only solution!

RAYMOND DOUGLAS STANFORD

63. Do you think it is possible to have too much sex? Do we? What should we do about it?

64. How do you feel about performing oral sex on me? How do you feel about receiving oral sex?

65. When performing oral sex on me, do you know what gives me pleasure?

66. How important is foreplay to you?

67. Where is the place to touch you that turns you on the most?

68. What part can lingerie play in our sexual relation-ship?

69. What is your favorite sex position?

70. Which methods of contraception are you most comfortable with?

71. After we get married, how often do you anticipate we will make love?

Sexual problems don't have to be fatal to your relationship, but they will be if you avoid dealing with them.

BARBARA DE ANGELIS,
ARE YOU THE ONE FOR ME?

Men as well as women are much oftener led by their hearts than by their understandings.

LORD CHESTERFIELD

72. Are you comfortable referring to the body parts of the opposite sex?

73. How important will sex be in our marriage?

74. What is a sensitive way for me to help you cope with the pain you may experience when first making love?

75. How important is romance to you?

76. Should sex be only for having children?

77. Is there anything sexually you would not do?

78. Do you feel that you are doing me a favor by making love to me, or are we celebrating our mutual love and affection for each other?

79. Does everything in life have to go your way for you to want to have sex with me?

80. How would impotence affect our relationship?

Divorces occur often over sex, money, and child discipline. If you study the divorces, as we have had to do in these past years, you will find that there are one, two, three, four reasons. Generally sex is the first. They did not get along sexually. They may not say that in the courtroom. They may not even tell that to their attorneys . . . but that is the reason!

SPENCER KIMBALL

81. How would our relationship be affected if for medical reasons we could not have children?

82. What is the best way to turn you on?

83. When would you prefer that I do not make sexual advances to you?

84. What do I do that sends you the message that I want sex?

85. How do you feel about not having sex with anyone else but me for the rest of your life?

86. Have you had any problems with your sexual relationship with any of your previous partners? If so, what were they?

87. Would you get tested for sexually transmitted diseases if I asked you?

88. What is desire?

89. Which side of the bed do you want to sleep on?

True, we love life, not because we are used to living, but because we are used to loving. There is always some madness in love, but there is always some reason in madness.

WOLFGANG AMADEUS MOZART

Immature love says: "I love you because I need you."
Mature love says: "I need you because I love you."

ERICH FROMM

90. What would you do if I had an affair?

91. Would it bother you if I had artificial breasts?

92. Are headaches or sore breasts going to be your way of saying get lost?

93. Generally speaking, do you want sex because of desire or habit?

94. Do you think I should be able to read your mind to determine what you want sexually?

95. Do you want me to call out your name during sex?

96. Do you prefer to talk or be quiet during sex?

97. Do you like to make noise during sex?

98. Are you comfortable having your eyes open during sex?

99. How do you feel about looking into my eyes during sex?

Every mother generally hopes that her daughter will snag a better husband than she managed to . . . but she's certain that her boy will never get as great a wife as his father did.

'Tis better to have loved and lost than never to have loved at all.

ALFRED, LORD TENNYSON

The course of true love never did run smooth.

WILLIAM SHAKESPEARE

100. Are you comfortable enough with your body to make love with the lights on?

101. How important is visual stimulation to you?

102. How do you feel about me discussing our sex lives with others?

103. Are there any particular sexual games that you like or want to experiment with?

104. Would you like to use mirrors to view our love-making from another angle?

105. How do you feel about making a home movie of our lovemaking?

106. Who should be responsible for contraception in our relationship?

107. How do you feel about taking showers together?

108. Do you think a woman should wear makeup when making love?

109. How old should our children be when we teach them about sex?

110. Does having a tan make you feel sexier?

111. How do you feel about immediately lighting up a cigarette after sex? How do you feel if your partner does it?

112. Should sex follow every date that we have?

113. Would you make love to me if you did not feel like it?

114. What is wrong with our sex life?

115. Are our sexual needs compatible?

116. Do you think our sexual intensity or regularity will change after we have been together for a while? Why? Does this bother you?

117. Why or why not do you feel the need to dress sexy?

118. Is one of us more sexually dominant than the other?

119. Are there advantages in having sex before marriage? With your marriage partner? With previous partners? What are they?

120. How can you help me become a better lover?

121. Is there anything you would like to change about your sexual prowess?

122. Do you want to be with me because I am the best sexual partner you have ever had? If I'm not, why do you want to be with me?

123. Could something occur in our relationship to cause us to be disinterested in each other sexually? What type of thing would it be?

124. Do you think kissing you is a sign that I want sex?

125. Do you believe you can learn to become a great lover?

126. Which days/times are best for us to make love?

127. Do you think exercising improves sexual performance?

128. What is your greatest sexual weakness?

129. Have you ever used sex as a tool to get what you want? When? Why?

130. Is sex a good way to celebrate the resolution of an argument?

131. Do you have sexual secrets? Would you ever be willing to share any of them?

132. Are you bisexual?

133. Do you think your affection for me is similar to the feelings your mother and father have for each other?

134. Do you resent me when I say I don't feel like making love?

135. When would you prefer that I not ask you for sex?

136. Do you feel pressured to make love to me?

137. Are the clothes you wear a reflection of your sexual personality?

138. Do you or will you talk about our sex lives with others?

139. Do you think sex should be confined to the bedroom?

140. Would you still respect me in the morning if I did something totally naughty in bed the night before?

141. Would you go to a sex therapist if I felt we needed to?

RELIGION
AND
SPIRITUALITY

Mankind is engaged in an eternal quest for that "something else" he hopes will bring him happiness, complete and unending. For those individual souls who have sought and found God, the search is over: He is that something else.

PARAMAHANSA YOGANANDA,
AUTOBIOGRAPHY OF A YOGI

1. What measures should we take before we get married to ensure that we maintain our religious beliefs concerning sex?

2. Whatever your religious choice, do you live it conscientiously?

3. What place do you believe religion will have in our lives?

4. If we have different religious beliefs, what problems might that present for our wedding, acquisition of material goods, or the way our future children will be raised?

5. Do you believe in ghosts?

6. Do you believe that we choose our own course in life or is it preordained?

7. Do you believe God has any influence over your being rich or poor?

8. How will our religion assist in maintaining harmony in our marriage?

9. Why is religion important or unimportant in your life?

10. What influence do your religious leaders have on your day-to-day life?

11. Do you believe religious leaders have the right to tell you what to do?

12. What is your attitude toward people with religious beliefs that differ from yours?

13. What place do you believe religion has in the world?

14. What has been your most negative experience with your religion or other religions?

15. What has been your most positive experience with your religion or other religions?

16. What is your interpretation of your religion's policy on contraception?

17. How often do you want to go to church?

We have pursued our masculine and extroverted values for so long, we have come to see the soul as an unnecessary complication in an otherwise neat and tidy masculine world.

ROBERT A. JOHNSON

Diseases of the soul are more dangerous and more numerous than those of the body.

CICERO

*I believe God sometimes tests our
faith. Sometimes God has a better plan
for us than we have for ourselves.*

THOMAS STANLEY, PH.D.,
THE MILLIONAIRE MIND

*Just think, if it weren't for marriage,
men would go through life thinking
they had no faults at all.*

UNKNOWN

18. What would cause you to stop going to church?

19. What importance should we place on sex before marriage?

20. If, after we got married, I drifted from the church of our mutual belief, how would that affect you? Would you still love me as you did before?

21. Do you believe we can go through life without God?

22. Have you done anything sinful that you need to get off your chest?

23. How does your belief in God aid you in coping with stress and challenges in life?

24. What is the purpose of your life?

25. Do you believe there are evil spiritual forces in the world?

26. Do you need religion to be close to God?

27. Where did we come from before we were born?

28. What happens to us when we die?

29. How do you feel about donations to charity?

30. How would you describe your spiritual self?

31. Do you believe in reincarnation?

32. Do you believe that there is only one true religion and all others are false?

33. Do you believe that Satan actually exists?

34. Which religion do you dislike the most and why?

35. How would you change the effect religion has on the world?

36. Do you believe that God is responsible for the good and bad things that happen in your life?

SELF-WORTH

The majority of divorce-causing problems are foreseeable before the wedding takes place.

However, it is not until couples marry that this realization surfaces. Moreover, individuals who marry again and again continue to repeat the same mistakes, never internalizing the principle that it is critical to know another person thoroughly before marriage takes place.

COREY DONALDSON

1. At this stage in our relationship, do you still feel the need to be on your best behavior, or are you comfortable being yourself?

2. Is your personal self-esteem related to having lots of money or material possessions?

3. What makes you feel important?

4. How do you maintain your self-esteem?

5. What causes you to lose your self-esteem?

6. On what occasion(s) have you admitted you were wrong?

7. Do you see yourself as emotionally stable or unstable?

8. Are you content in your own company?

9. What do you think about when you have nothing specific to think about?

10. What is your most negative characteristic? What are you doing about it?

11. Do you accept criticism easily?

12. What is the best way to accept a compliment?

13. Have you ever found yourself putting others down to make yourself feel better? If so, is that fair? If you believe you don't do it to make yourself feel better, why do you do it?

14. Do you believe you are a self-starter?

15. Does it matter to you who earns most of the money?

16. When have you succumbed to peer pressure? If you could relive those occasions, would you behave differently?

17. Are you selfish? When? Why? What are you doing about it?

18. What makes you feel lonely?

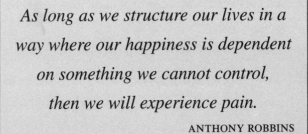

*As long as we structure our lives in a
way where our happiness is dependent
on something we cannot control,
then we will experience pain.*

ANTHONY ROBBINS

*Self-esteem in a mate is a fragile
flower. It can be crushed so easily!*

DR. JAMES DOBSON

19. Do you see yourself as worthy of love? Why or why not?

20. What do you dislike about being single?

21. Do you believe that "wholeness" as a person is related to being with a partner, or is achieving it a separate and distinct personal quest undertaken by an individual?

22. Have you ever felt, or do you now feel, pressure to marry?

23. Are you comfortable in a social setting where you meet people for the first time?

24. Do you have the ability to initiate and carry on a conversation with a person you just met?

25. How often do you want to socialize with others after we are married?

26. Have you ever thought that you should marry me because if you don't, no one else will come along, and you will be lonely for the rest of your life?

Making Love (may-king-luv) n.

Female: The greatest expression of intimacy a couple can achieve.

Male: Call it whatever you want just as long as we end up in bed.

UNKNOWN

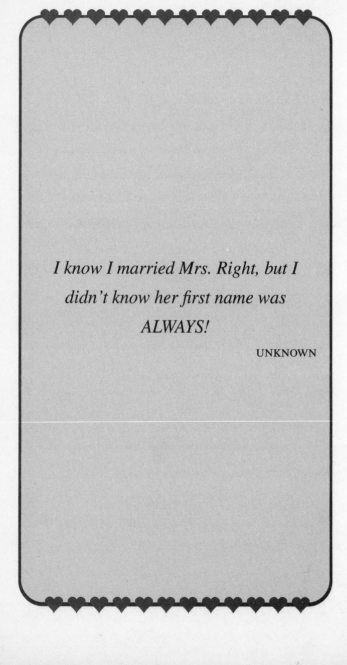

I know I married Mrs. Right, but I didn't know her first name was ALWAYS!

UNKNOWN

27. When your self-esteem is low, are you liable to do or think things you normally wouldn't?

28. What makes you think you are good enough to marry me?

29. Is it possible that we are getting married because somehow it will make us more secure in our relationship? Why don't we just live together?

30. Are you comfortable with the way your body looks?

31. What do you dislike about yourself?

32. If you were to die today, what would people say about you at your funeral?

33. How often do you talk about yourself?

34. Do you sense that others may think that you talk too much about yourself?

35. What is the most exciting aspect of your life?

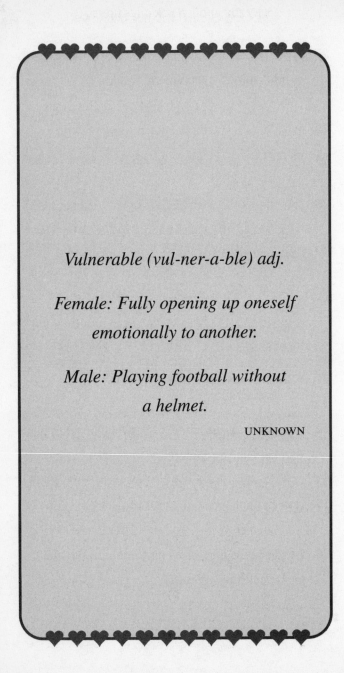

Vulnerable (vul-ner-a-ble) adj.

Female: Fully opening up oneself emotionally to another.

Male: Playing football without a helmet.

UNKNOWN

36. What do you see as being your needs in a marriage?

37. Do you feel the need to flirt with others? Why?

38. If you had to describe yourself in ten words, what would they be?

39. How important is it to you that everyone likes you?

40. Does having new clothes, good hair, or "nice things" give you more self-esteem?

41. What are your sexual insecurities and are they linked to self-esteem?

42. Is there a link between the amount of sex you have and your self-esteem?

43. To what degree does sex make you feel loved?

EXPECTATIONS

If your focus is on the attributes in your partner that you like, without regard to the attributes you dislike, you are a fool!

COREY DONALDSON

1. Do you feel that I accept you as you are, or do you think that there are things about you that I want to change?

2. If we had agreed to wait to have children and you, the female partner, decided on your own that you wanted children and stopped using birth control and then got pregnant, how would you expect me to react? If you're male, how would you react?

3. Are there duties you expect me to carry out that you would not do?

4. What do you expect from me as your future spouse? Do you believe your expectations are fair? Why?

5. What does commitment mean to you?

6. What purpose do you believe I will serve in our marriage?

7. What is your attitude toward people who disagree with you?

Your focus should not be "What can my partner do for me?" but "What can I do for my partner?"

COREY DONALDSON

It is likely that whatever challenges you face in life could have been avoided by some better decisions upstream.

ANTHONY ROBBINS

All people are liars until proven otherwise!

BARRY DONALDSON

8. How often do you expect us to be with your family after we are married?

9. Do you behave differently with different people?

10. Do you feel the need to be nurtured by another who is emotionally or physically stronger? Why or why not?

11. Who will be the predominant breadwinner?

12. How long do you want to wait before having children?

13. Who will wash the dishes, clean the bathroom, vacuum the carpet, clean the car, take out the garbage, cook, make the bed, tidy the house, clean the kitchen, bathe and dress the children, change diapers, drop children at school, pick children up from school, and do the shopping? How often?

14. How important is a clean and tidy home to you?

15. Would your feelings toward me change if I were unemployed for a long time?

16. What do you fear in relationships?

17. What do you expect of me sexually?

18. How often do you expect to buy new clothes after we are married?

19. Do you always expect to be right?

20. Why is it important for us to act as if we are still dating after we are married?

21. If we are eating a block of chocolate together and there is one piece left, who gets it?

22. Do you expect me to tolerate your bad habits?

23. What bad habits do you expect to overcome in the next twelve months?

THE PAST

*When you bring things out in others
that they like about themselves, they'll
believe your relationship is healthy.
The same is true in reverse. When they
bring out things that you like best in
you, you'll think the relationship is
healthy. When this occurs, bonding
takes place.*

MARSHALL SYLVER,
PASSION, PROFIT AND POWER

1. Which childhood experiences influence your behavior and attitudes the most?

2. Could any feelings of affection and romance be revived if you met a previous boyfriend/girlfriend even though you feel strongly committed to me?

3. As you were growing up, did you think more about the type of person you wanted to marry, or the type of person you wanted to be for your spouse? Why? Describe your thoughts.

4. Do you feel the need to maintain relationships with your past boyfriends/girlfriends? Why or why not? If these relationships made me feel uncomfortable, would you end them for me?

5. How is our relationship different from or similar to the ones you have had in the past?

6. Is there anything in your past I should be aware of?

7. What did you dislike most about previous partners?

8. What are you most grateful for?

The more a man talks to you about his past, the more likely he will speak about his future.

MARGARET KENT,
HOW TO MARRY THE MAN
OF YOUR CHOICE

9. Have you ever blamed others when things are going wrong for you?

10. What did you like or dislike most about your childhood?

11. What has made you angry about the past?

12. What did your mother or father do when you were growing up that you wish I would do?

13. If your past boyfriends/girlfriends listed your most negative characteristics, what would they be?

14. Do you keep letters and memorabilia from past relationships? Why or why not?

15. Are you comfortable continuing this relationship if there are things in my past that I am not willing to share with you?

16. What is your favorite pastime?

17. What was your most embarrassing moment?

18. Do you now feel or have you ever felt that there might be something in our future relationship that could cause friction?

19. What has been your greatest disappointment in life?

20. Would it concern you if I had had sex with others out of wedlock in the past? Would you want to know regardless of how long ago it happened?

21. Are there any disagreements from the past that we have not yet resolved?

22. Have you ever cheated on a past girlfriend/boyfriend? If so, what is your plan for never doing it again, and why should I believe you would never cheat on me?

23. Do you still have affectionate feelings for any previous partner?

24. When you were a child or teenager, did your family encourage discussing feelings, or was your home a suppressive environment?

Success in marriage is much more than a matter of finding the right person; it is also a matter of being the right person.

LELAND FOSTER WOOD

A few seem to extract from their childhood the skills and motivation that allow them, as adults, to make extraordinary achievements. Some remain trapped by events that occurred long ago.

CLAIR CARMICHAEL,
GETTING IT RIGHT

So many self-inflict life-crushing blows as they turn a blind eye to the lessons of the past. To ignore the negative experience of one's own life or that of another invites heartache to recycle throughout life.

COREY DONALDSON

25. Did your mother or father abuse each other or you in any way—sexually, emotionally, or physically?

26. What have you learned from relationships between other couples?

27. Why have you ended a relationship in the past?

28. Considering what your life has been like thus far, what do you think your future will be like? Will it be the same or different? Please explain.

29. Do you define yourself by what you've done in the past or by your ongoing and consistent achievements?

30. If I talked to your ex(es), what warnings would they give me about you?

31. What mistakes have you made in previous relationships?

32. Have you ever been involved in any criminal activities? What were they?

Finding someone who fills an unmet childhood need is often such a relief that a person will stay in an otherwise unrewarding relationship because of fear of losing what has been gained.

CLAIR CARMICHAEL

33. Are you involved in any criminal activities right now?

34. Have you ever been to prison? Why?

35. Have you ever been able to overcome a bad habit? What was it?

36. What are the four most powerful experiences that have helped make you who you are today?

37. Have you ever been violent in past relationships?

38. Has anyone ever had cause to be afraid of you?

39. What is your deepest, darkest secret?

40. Has anyone ever taken naked pictures of you?

41. Have you ever had sex with someone you did not know very well?

42. How many times have you had a one-night stand?

43. How many men/women have you slept with?

Contrary to what the dictionary tells us, pretending is potentially the most serious form of deception because it can involve living a lie, rather then telling one.

HARRIET LERNER, PH.D.,
THE DANCE OF DECEPTION

44. Have you ever been committed to a mental hospital or been treated for a mental illness?

45. Have you ever misrepresented yourself on your taxes?

46. What did you like most about me when we first met?

47. Have you ever been served with a summons or a subpoena?

48. Have you ever been in a porn film?

49. Is there something about you that you hope I never find out?

50. Is there a history of alcoholism or any other substance abuse in your family?

51. Have you ever been arrested?

52. Have you ever had unprotected sex with a person you did not know very well?

TRUST

A wife is one who shares her husband's thoughts, incorporates his heart with hers in love, and crowns him with her trust.

HENRY VAN DYKE

1. Is my opinion more important to you than what others think?

2. If there is one thing you could do but are not currently doing to make our relationship more meaningful, what is it? Will you do it?

3. Have there been times when you were uncomfortable with the way I behaved with the opposite sex? If so, when, and what did I do?

4. When every couple is married, the partners make vows never to have sexual relations with any other person. How is it, then, that so many break these vows? What are the measures you can take to avoid this happening in our relationship?

5. What do (1) respect, (2) loyalty, (3) honesty, (4) love, (5) emotional intimacy, and (6) trust mean to you? Why are these qualities important?

6. What does monogamy mean to you?

Happy marriages are rarely the product of chance: They are architectural in that they are intelligently and deliberately planned.

DR. BUTTERFIELD

A lasting love is based on knowledge, not assumptions and wishes. If to know him is to love him, your love will be real.

MARGARET KENT

It is better to dwell in a corner of the housetop than with a brawling woman in a wide house.

PROVERBS 21:9

7. Do you feel there are issues between us that should be kept confidential even from our children? If so, what are they?

8. If you are ever tempted to cheat on me, how will you deal with the situation?

9. How would you react if I cheated on you?

10. What do I do now, or what could I do in the future, that would make you mistrust me?

11. Would you be comfortable transferring all your money into my bank account?

12. If one of my best friends is a member of the opposite sex and very attractive, would it bother you if I spent time with him/her?

13. Has there ever been a time when you were disloyal to a previous partner?

14. What reasons have people ever had to mistrust you?

When an affair starts, it begins as a friendship. You share problems with the other person, and that person shares problems with you. Usually, for the affair to blossom, you have to see this other person quite often: every day at work or frequently through a friendship, being on a committee or board, or some other responsibility that brings you together. . . . Not uncommonly, the third party is either the husband or wife in a couple you both know and consider "best friends." In another common pattern, the outside lover comes from your spouse's family—a sister or brother.

WILLARD F. HARLEY JR.

15. Why do you feel that you are trustworthy?

16. Who comes first, your spouse or your children?

17. How would you feel if my ex rang me constantly to discuss children, child support, bills, or just casually to talk?

18. How is trust earned?

19. Is trust automatic until something occurs that takes it away, or does it evolve over time?

20. What amount of contact with my ex is acceptable, and for what reasons?

21. In what ways is it or isn't it a satisfying experience when you come to me for advice?

22. Do you trust me with money?

23. Are you jealous?

24. Would you take a phone number from another woman/man in a social setting?

25. How do you feel about me going to a dance/night-club without you?

26. How would it make you feel if I danced with others?

27. If I worked in theater, TV, or modeling and had to kiss someone, how would that affect you?

28. If my work involved dressing provocatively or wearing nothing at all, how would that affect you?

29. What is and what is not cheating?

30. How would you feel about me talking with others about you?

31. Is it permissible for us to open each other's mail?

32. Is it cheating to flirt with someone on the Internet?

33. Do you trust me enough to share your sexual history with me?

THE FUTURE

Sadly, we live in a society where far too many people die years before they are buried.

TAYLOR HARTMAN, PH.D.,
THE COLOR CODE

1. Do you think seriously about our future, or do you just take it for granted that all will be fine?

2. In what ways are we different? Could this be a source of future conflict? Do our differences complement each other?

3. Do you anticipate maintaining your single lifestyle after we are married? That is, will you spend just as much time with your friends, family, and work colleagues? Why or why not?

4. If we could see into the future, and knew that children would reduce the affection and passion in our relationship, would you still want to have children?

5. If we are unable to have children, should we adopt?

6. How did your family resolve conflicts when you were growing up? Do you approve or disapprove of that method? What will you change or not change to resolve conflicts in your future family?

7. What types of discipline would you implement to correct a child's or teenager's behavior? Were these

practices you experienced, or are they new ones you have developed on your own?

8. If you had to choose between me or your best friend because of some unreasonable conflict, what would you do? Why?

9. Is there anything about marriage that frightens you?

10. Would you prefer to live in the city, the country, or by the beach? Why?

11. If I wanted to move away from our families for work, would you support me? Why?

12. Can you recognize that at times you may be mad at me when really an external factor has ignited your anger? Is it possible this could happen in the future? If this has happened or could happen, do you believe it is fair? What strategy will you implement to prevent it from occurring?

13. If you had the opportunity to live your entire life again, what would you do differently?

*A good marriage is simply the union of
"two awfully good forgivers." . . . To
forgive is to put the offense away
completely.*

CAROLE MAYHALL

*Anyone can become angry—that is
easy. But to be angry with the right
person, to the right degree, at the right
time, for the right purpose, and in the
right way—this is not easy.*

ARISTOTLE

Anger is never without a reason, but seldom a good one.

BENJAMIN FRANKLIN

Communication

(ko-myoo-ni-kay-shon) n.

Female: The open sharing of thoughts and feelings with one's partner.

Male: Scratching out a note before suddenly taking off for a weekend with the boys.

UNKNOWN

14. Do you anticipate raising our children (1) the same way you were raised, (2) completely differently from the way you were raised, or (3) a mixture of both?

15. How long would you like to wait before having children?

16. What changes do you expect to occur in your life after we are married?

17. How would it affect you if I traveled on my own frequently to (1) visit family, (2) earn income, (3) pursue a hobby, or (4) deal with stress?

18. What does it mean to give 100 percent of yourself in marriage?

19. Would you be willing to move away from family and friends to follow (1) my career, (2) your career, (3) both of our careers?

20. Suppose we are experiencing trouble in our marriage. In what order will you seek help from the following to resolve our conflicts: (1) divorce lawyer, (2) your parents, (3) a brother or sister, (4) a marriage counselor, (5) me, (6) an ecclesiastical leader? Why?

21. If you felt left out because I was giving too much attention to our child or pet, what would you do?

22. Could you live away from your parents for more than one year?

23. Why do you want or not want children?

24. What differences are there in our characters that could cause incompatibility in the future? How should we handle these differences?

● 25. How would your feelings toward me change if I gained weight?

26. Have we spent enough time together to justify a lifetime with each other?

27. Do you have the right to discipline *my* children? In what ways?

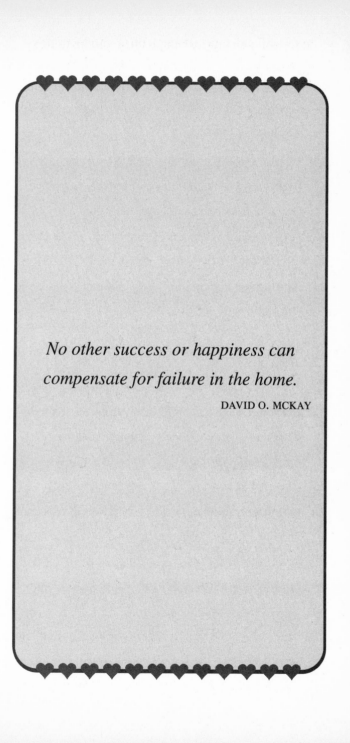

*No other success or happiness can
compensate for failure in the home.*

DAVID O. MCKAY

28. What are your child-support/custody arrangements with your ex?

29. What is a warning sign that a child could be planning on a violent act against us or some other person?

30. How would you address violent behavior in a child?

31. At what age do you think our children should be allowed to single-date?

32. What part will education play in our lives?

33. Do you believe that children should choose freely whether to go to college, without the influence/ pressure of parents?

34. Other than formal schooling, what types of education will our children get and how will they receive them?

35. Once we are married, how do you see our relation- ship evolving/changing?

36. How important is it to you that your children share your hobbies?

The husband who wants a happy marriage should keep his mouth shut and his checkbook open.

GROUCHO MARX

I would give up all my genius, and all my books, if there were only some woman, somewhere, who cared whether or not I came home late for dinner.

IVAN TURGENEV

37. Would it hurt your feelings if your children did not like the recreational activities that you like?

38. When we have children, who will change the diapers, make the bottle, prepare meals, do the housework, bathe the child, get up in the middle of the night when the child is crying, take the child to the doctor, buy the clothing, and dress the child? Who will have the most patience with these responsibilities?

39. How will you support my hobbies?

40. How will we incorporate religion into our children's lives?

41. How do you feel about having our parents come to live with us if the need arises?

42. What do you look forward to?

43. What are your dreams for the future?

44. Which new responsibilities do you see yourself taking on in the next five years, and how are you preparing to meet those responsibilities?

45. How could the jobs we have affect our children?

46. How do you think I would handle it if our child had a tantrum?

47. Is there anything you would regret not being able to do or accomplish if you married me?

48. How many vacations do you want to take each year once we are married?

49. How do you feel about going on weekend getaways?

50. What is your vision of us when we are old?

51. What attitude do you want our children to have about fighting?

52. How would you feel about a relative moving in with us?

53. Whose family will we celebrate the holidays with?

54. Will the discipline and raising of our children be a joint and consistent effort regardless of who they are?

ANNOYANCES

When you learn to feel people with your heart and not just see them with your eyes, you will attract much more compatible partners into your life.

BARBARA DE ANGELIS

1. Have you ever found yourself denying something you don't like about me, thinking it will go away or that you are overreacting?

2. If I call you by special names like darling, love, babe, or sweetie, would it bother you if I used these same names when talking to others of the opposite sex? Why?

3. How would it affect you if I criticized you or was sarcastic to you around other people?

4. If I have bad breath or body odor or wear dirty clothes, will you tell me? Should I tell you? Why or why not? How will we do it?

5. What is nagging? Do you think I nag? How does nagging make you feel?

6. When do you need to exercise a lot of patience with me?

7. Have you ever felt that I take you for granted? When?

People may or may not say what they mean . . . but they always say something designed to get what they want.

DAVID MAMET

If I were the devil . . .
I would attack the family, the backbone of any nation.
I would make divorce acceptable and easy, even fashionable. If the family crumbles, so does the nation.

PAUL HARVEY

8. Does it affect your ego if I disagree with you?

9. How does it affect you if I flirt with the opposite sex?

10. What is your definition of flirting?

11. Do you approve without reservation of the way I dress?

12. In your estimation, why do most couples break up?

13. What does my family do that annoys you?

14. What about men or women in general really annoys you?

15. How do I annoy you?

16. What things does your ex do to annoy you that you hope I never do?

17. When we are driving together, who will drive?

One of the most important ways to manifest integrity is to be loyal to those who are not present. In doing so, we build the trust of those who are present.

STEPHEN R. COVEY

18. Would it bother you if I made body noises all the time, like passing gas and burping?

19. Is there anything you do in your line of work that I would disapprove of or that would hurt me?

20. At what point in a marriage do you feel divorce is appropriate (or inevitable)?

21. Do you believe that you should stick with a marriage if you are unhappy all the time?

22. Have you ever been hurt in a relationship to the point that you made a personal vow to get back at your partner?

23. Do you like pets?

24. Would you allow pets in the bedroom or let them sleep in the bed?

25. Does my nose hair bother you?

26. Do you feel you could communicate with me under any circumstances and about any subject?

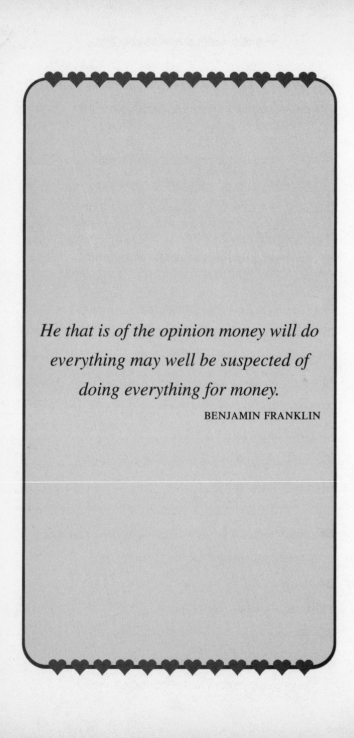

He that is of the opinion money will do everything may well be suspected of doing everything for money.

BENJAMIN FRANKLIN

27. Do you think being in love means (1) never having to say you're sorry, (2) always having to say you're sorry, (3) knowing when to say you're sorry, or (4) being the first to say I am sorry?

28. How would you describe my sense of humor?

29. If you had doubts about our relationship, would you say so?

30. Is there anything we have not discussed that concerns you about our relationship?

31. What do you not like about me?

32. What do you like or not like about our dates together?

33. Would you care if I had yellow teeth?

34. How forgiving are you?

35. Do you think I take life too seriously?

36. When do you need space away from me?

37. Do you ever feel your temper is uncontrollable?

38. Do you worry about violent inclinations in yourself?

39. Have you ever been so angry that you became violent? What happened? What did you do to deal with the problem?

40. Do you snore?

41. Do you leave the toilet seat up?

42. Would you have dinner with a former lover even though you knew I was against it?

43. How often do you shower?

44. Do you promise not to roll your eyes when I tell new people the same story that you've heard a thousand times?

45. Will it bother you if I use the bathroom with the door open?

46. When taking your clothes off at the end of the day, do you hang them up neatly or leave them on the floor?

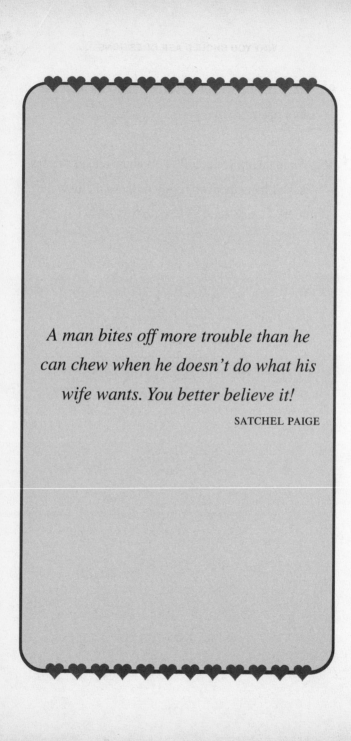

A man bites off more trouble than he can chew when he doesn't do what his wife wants. You better believe it!

SATCHEL PAIGE

In the world of romance, one single rule applies:

Make the woman happy.

Do something she likes, and you get points.

Do something she dislikes, and points are subtracted.

You don't get any points for doing something she

expects. Sorry, that's the way the game is played.

Social Engagements:

Party: You stay by her side the entire party 0

You stay by her side for a while, then leave to chat

with a college drinking buddy . . . . . . –2

Named Tiffany . . . . . . –4

Tiffany is a dancer . . . . . . –6

Tiffany has implants . . . . . . –8

Her Birthday:

You take her out to dinner 0

You take her out to dinner

and it's not a sports bar . . . . . . +1

Okay, it's a sports bar . . . . . . –2

And it's all-you-can-eat night . . . . . . –3

It's a sports bar, it's all-you-can-eat night, and your

face is painted the colors of your

favorite team . . . . . . –10

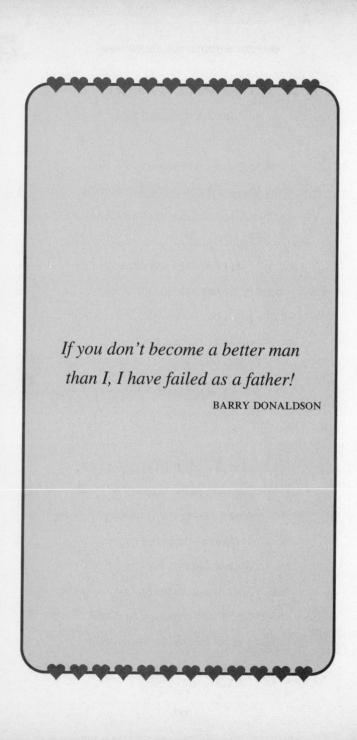

If you don't become a better man

than I, I have failed as a father!

BARRY DONALDSON

A Night Out with the Boys:

Go with a pal . . . . . . –5

The pal is happily married . . . . . . –4

Or frighteningly single . . . . . . –7

And he drives a Mustang . . . . . . –10

With a personalized license plate

(GR8 N BED) . . . . . . –15

A Night Out:

You take her to a movie . . . . . . +2

You take her to a movie she likes . . . . . . +4

You take her to a movie you hate . . . . . . +6

You take her to a movie you like . . . . . . –2

It's called *DeathCop 3* . . . . . . –3

And features cyborgs that eat humans . . . . . . –9

You lied and said it was a foreign film

about orphans . . . . . . –15

The Big Question:

She asks, "Do I look fat?"

You hesitate in responding . . . . . . –10

You reply, "Where?" . . . . . . –35

Any other response . . . . . . –20

UNKNOWN

47. Would it bother you if I danced with other people, in or out of your presence?

48. How would you feel about my best friend visiting us every day?

49. Are you gay but marrying me to cover it up?

50. Must I watch the movies you like with you?

51. Do you replace the toilet-paper roll as soon as it is used up?

52. Do you get mad when people disagree with you?

53. Would you be uncomfortable if I walked around the house naked?

54. How do you feel about me maintaining my previous sexual partners as friends?

55. Would it annoy you if I talked about previous sexual experiences with others?

COMMUNICATION

Let the husband render unto the wife

due benevolence.

I CORINTHIANS 7:3

1. What is the best way for me to communicate difficult feelings about you so that you are not offended? Is it possible to do this at all?

2. Whenever we have difficult feelings about each other, should we (1) remain silent, (2) say something as soon as the difficult feelings arise, (3) wait a certain amount of time before raising the issue, or (4) do something else? If so, what?

3. If I ever feel a need to give you positive reinforcement (criticism), what is the best way?

4. If you always say you are going to do something but never do it, what is the most effective way to bring this problem to your attention?

5. If we are with other people and I express an opinion that everyone, including you, disagrees with, do you (1) join them, (2) wait for us to be alone before you express your feelings, (3) pretend to agree with me, or (4) take some other action? Why?

6. When you think about the way you communicate with me, which of these do you consider: (1) the

Some parents don't realize that even a loud tone of voice or a comment that is amusing to an adult about the child's inadequacies can be devastating, particularly when this happens in public.

CLAIR CARMICHAEL

words you speak, (2) your tone of voice, (3) your body language, (4) your facial expression, (5) your silence, (6) your sarcasm, (7) your humor, (8) all of these elements?

7. Why is effective communication important in a marriage?

8. What did you admire about the way your mother and father treated each other?

9. What are some possible barriers to effective communication?

10. What excuses are there for you and I to raise our voices to each other?

11. If I want you to do something for me within a given time, what is the best way to ask you without making me sound demanding or like a nag?

12. Is there anything about men or women that you have had difficulty understanding in the past?

Romantic love is the single greatest energy system in the Western psyche. In our culture it has supplanted religion as the arena in which men and women seek meaning, transcendence, wholeness, and ecstasy.

ROBERT A. JOHNSON

13. What do you fear about communicating your feelings?

14. Is there anything about the discussion of feelings that makes you uncomfortable?

15. If we are unable to communicate our feelings or thoughts effectively to each other, should we seek counseling?

16. When we have an argument, will you go to your friends and family for solutions/comfort or seek the solution/comfort within our relationship?

17. Who should know about the arguments we have?

18. If your stepson/stepdaughter dislikes you for reasons that you don't know and he/she does not want to talk to you, how will you deal with it?

19. Generally speaking, when your mom and dad have an argument, who is right? Why?

20. What makes you not want to talk to me?

Of all the surefire, infernal devices ever invented by all the devils in hell for destroying love, nagging is the deadliest. It never fails. Like the bite of the king cobra, it always destroys, always kills.

DALE CARNEGIE,
HOW TO WIN FRIENDS AND
INFLUENCE PEOPLE

21. How do you feel about expressing your feelings through crying?

22. Should I feel threatened or worried if you say, "We have to talk"?

MONEY

For every ten coins thou placest within
thy purse, take out for use but nine.
Thy purse will start to fatten at once
and its increasing weight will feel good
in thy hand and bring satisfaction
to thy soul.

GEORGE S. CLASON,
THE RICHEST MAN IN BABYLON

1. Financially, do you plan to (1) just get by, (2) have a little extra spending money, (3) be independent, (4) be wealthy, or (5) not know what our financial situation will be like? Why? How do you plan to achieve your goal?

2. What justifies going into debt?

3. What are all your current personal debts?

4. Do you feel stress when facing financial problems? How do you deal with that stress?

5. Are we going to rent? For how long?

6. What do you know about mortgages, interest rates, and applying for loans?

7. What do you know about investments in property or stocks and bonds?

8. How often do you use credit cards, and what do you buy with them?

9. How should we prepare for a financial emergency?

10. Do you feel that lack of money is a good reason not to have children?

11. How is your credit rating?

12. Should our children pay for their own college?

13. When our child is born, will he or she go to day care, or will one of us stay home to take care of the child? Who will it be?

14. Will we have a budget? What will it be?

15. How will we decide what money is mine, yours, or ours?

16. Who will pay the bills?

17. How do you feel about helping me pay my debts and bills?

18. How much extra money do you think I should give to my ex to support my children?

19. Are you a good loan risk?

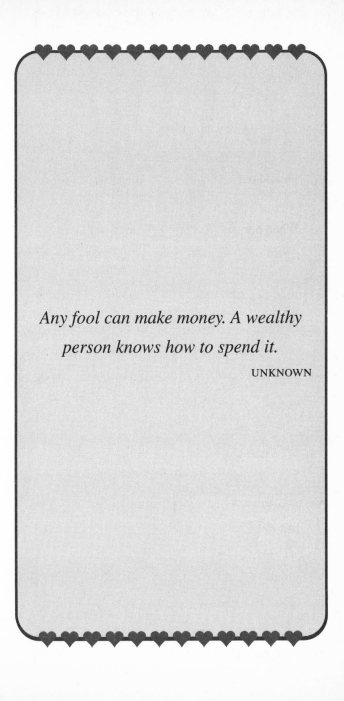

Any fool can make money. A wealthy

person knows how to spend it.

UNKNOWN

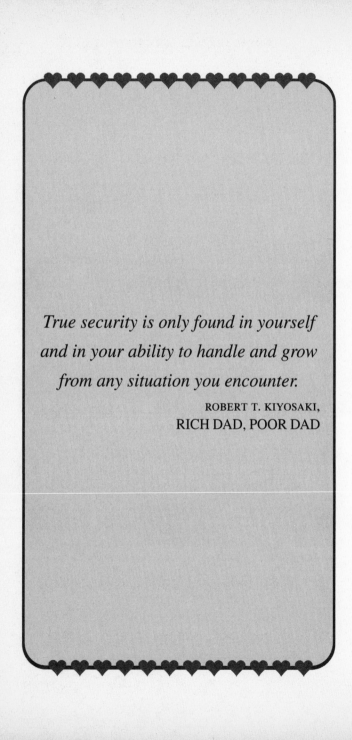

True security is only found in yourself and in your ability to handle and grow from any situation you encounter.

ROBERT T. KIYOSAKI,
RICH DAD, POOR DAD

20. Are your feelings for me dependent on my always having money?

21. How do you feel about having a very small wedding so that we can take the money we would have spent on a big wedding and put it toward a house?

22. How do you feel about borrowing money from each other before we get married?

23. Have you ever sued someone or been sued? What were the circumstances?

24. What are your feelings about saving money?

25. Do you pay credit cards off at the end of the month or do you carry a balance?

26. What is your dream car?

27. Who will balance our checkbook?

28. Do you prefer separate bank accounts or assets in different names? Why?

The difference between what you know and what you don't know about your partner is the questions you ask.

COREY DONALDSON

AND DON'T FORGET TO ASK...

When 733 millionaires were surveyed to identify the factors that most determined their success, having a supportive spouse *ranked as number 4 on a list of 30.*

THOMAS J. STANLEY, PH.D.,
THE MILLIONAIRE MIND

1. What makes you think we are right for each other?

2. How would you rank all the priorities in your life: work, school, family, spouse, friends, hobbies, and church? Does your ranking reflect the amount of time you spend on each?

3. Which would have the most lasting negative effect on you: (1) a failed marriage, (2) failure in your career, (3) a child disowning you, or (4) bankruptcy? Why?

4. Is anything more important to you than your spouse? If so, what is it? If not, does that mean you would sacrifice anything to preserve your relationship?

5. Do you believe household responsibilities should be divided according to the sex of each partner? Why or why not?

6. If I ask you to spend more time with me and less with your friends, sports, TV, or other family members, will you do it? Why not?

The rich acquire assets (assets put money in your pocket), the poor and middle class acquire liabilities (liabilities take money out of your pocket)!

ROBERT T. KIYOSAKI,
RICH DAD, POOR DAD

7. Why is family important to you?

8. Are you closer to your mother or father? Why?

9. If your mother or father issued a warning to me about you, what would it be? Would your best friend issue the same warning, or would the advice be different? How?

10. Do you think it is correct to believe that if someone has offended one of us, that person has offended both of us?

11. Do you prefer a set daily work schedule or flexible work activities and timetables?

12. Do you believe you are primarily an emotional or a logical thinker? Can you think of any examples?

13. What is right or wrong with feminism?

14. What is right or wrong with most men and women?

15. How do you believe men and women are different?

Phillip Blumstein and Pepper Schwartz's 1970 landmark study, American Couples, *found that couples who combined and shared their money were more likely to think of their marriages as permanent covenants. Those who believed marriage could be something less than a lifetime commitment were less apt to pool their funds.*

MARG STARK,
WHAT NO ONE TELLS THE BRIDE

16. Are there certain types of movies you refuse to see?

17. What do you fear?

18. What influence, if any, do you believe my family should have on our relationship?

19. Do you believe that our parents should know our financial condition, whether good or bad, just because they want to? How far should this go?

20. If you could receive any gift in the world, what would you choose?

21. If you could give any gift in the world, what would you choose, and to whom would you give it?

22. What efforts, if any, have you made to understand and accept my feelings and individuality?

23. Do you believe children should be seen and not heard? Why or why not?

24. What is your opinion of homosexuality?

Probably the worst thing about a prenuptial agreement is that it becomes, in many cases, a self-fulfilling prophecy. People who have prenups seem predisposed to divorce.

DONALD TRUMP,
THE ART OF THE COMEBACK

Marriage isn't a process of prolonging a life of love, but of mummifying the corpse.

P. G. WODEHOUSE

25. Do you believe in capital punishment?

26. What are your political views? How do you decide who to vote for?

27. What are your views on abortion?

28. What are your views on pornography?

29. How would you react if our eighteen-year-old son or daughter came home one night and told us he/she was gay?

30. Have you ever suppressed your feelings on a particular issue because you were afraid that if you shared them with me, I would not want to be with you anymore?

31. What kind of marriage will we have?

32. Do you harbor any racial prejudice?

33. How do you feel about having guns in our home?

*When woman acknowledges the good
in man, men can be freed from the fear
of the devouring feminine; when men
acknowledge the power in women,
woman can be freed from
the patriarchal prison.*

PAUL TOSCANO,
STRANGERS IN PARADOX

*The great question . . . which I have not
been able to answer, despite my thirty
years of research into the feminine
soul, is "What does a woman want?"*

SIGMUND FREUD

34. Have you ever had a gay experience?

35. Do you have gay feelings that you are suppressing?

36. How do you feel about socializing with gay people?

37. Is there anyone close to you who feels we should not get married? Why? Should we discuss this?

38. What would make you feel that I bore you in our relationship?

39. How do you think violence in schools can be stopped?

40. What is the most important aspect of keeping a relationship strong?

41. How often do you drink alcohol?

42. What are you like when you wake up in the morning?

43. Do you prefer to stay in or go out?

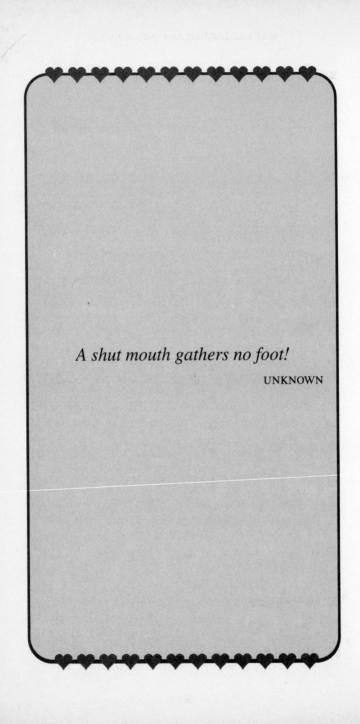

A shut mouth gathers no foot!

UNKNOWN

44. If you rented three videos, what would they be?

45. How many times a week do you like to eat out?

46. If I were in a lineup with ten other women/men where you could see only our feet, would you recognize mine?

47. Would you lose weight if I asked you to?

48. What is your greatest challenge in life?

49. As a couple, what is our highest common goal?

50. Who or what do you love?

51. Do we have more pain or pleasure in this relationship?

52. Do you suffer from a sleeping disorder?

53. What health problems do you have?

54. Have you ever had any psychological problems?

55. Have you ever been in a serious physical fight? What is your attitude toward fighting?

56. Describe your dream home.

57. Are you on any medication?

58. If we have two cars, who gets to drive the newer one?

59. Who would be your lifelines on *Who Wants to Be a Millionaire*?

60. What would cause you to want plastic surgery?

61. If our child was diagnosed with a severe defect early into pregnancy, would you go through with the birth?

62. If there is one issue that could cause us to divorce, what is it, and how will we ensure that it does not lead to a divorce?

SHOULD WE STILL GET MARRIED?

If you have decided to marry, you will realize by now that the future harmony of your relationship depends on how well you compromise and what allowances you make to accept and live with differences. It is too high an ideal to believe that you will always be in harmony. How comforting it is, however, to know beforehand what the confrontational issues will be. It allows you to deal with problems before they arise, so you can prevent disrupting your relationship as much as possible.

Perhaps after posing these questions to each other, you now feel it would be better to part. Don't you feel fortunate to have reached this decision now, rather than after getting married? Whatever your conclusion, always remember what you have learned and apply it in your future relationship(s), but please do not search for perfection; you will never find it.

If you are feeling unsure about what you should do, then you may not be ready for a commitment. Sometimes you need to take a look at yourself and take responsibility for what is going on in your mind. Only you can determine if you have cold feet or genuine concerns. Whatever the case may be, do not succumb to the pressure of getting married when your mind is in disarray. Many marry believing that annoying behaviors and attitudes will eventually change. Such fantasies sow the seeds of disillusionment, frustration, and even betrayal. This is a scenario that should be avoided at all costs. Ideally a marriage should take place when both partners accept each other's differences and feel that a foundation has been established to deal with those differences in the future.

The serious work of a courtship should never be undermined by cheap rhetoric or dismissed as unnecessary. The very foundation of your marriage is laid during this critical time. The strength with which you can with-decision to love, humor, infidelity and hard times, love and romance, myths, roles, sex, the stages of marriage, and successful marriage. This site features tests and quizzes, and much more.

www.helpself.com   Self-help quizzes that test your thinking, emotional state, emotional IQ (love, anger, etc.), or spirituality are found here. Give yourself the psychology tests.

www.seductionpalace.com   This site helps you to pop the question creatively. There are romantic cards to send; send a virtual kiss, and get ideas for spoiling your beloved.

www.ru4romance.com   This site is dedicated to putting the fun, the charm, and the romance back into dating. That means the spine-tingling enchantment of old-fashioned romance! But this time there's an innovative new twist. . . . The ladies are in control! *This is where you will find the Secret Admirer's Kit!* It gives ladies an intriguing prepackaged, do-it-yourself method to entice "your special man" into a mysterious romantic rendezvous!

www.armory.com/tests/purity.html   Although this is an unusual website by a self-proclaimed geek, it features tests that may be worthwhile as a tool for self-discovery.

SPEAKING AVAILABILITY

Corey Donaldson is available to speak at your location. As the author of *Don't You Dare Get Married Until You Read This,* he is a sought-out speaker on the topic of asking the right questions before marriage. His personal style, Australian charm, and candidness are sure to make him a hit with your audience as they come to a realization of what it really takes to make the right marriage choice.

For more information contact Corey Donaldson directly at cphaid@aol.com or at P.O. Box 13406, Ogden, Utah 84412-3406.

stand difficult times during marriage will be measured to a large extent by the way you shape your courtship.

As you approach this pivotal point in your life, I trust you will devote generous effort and energy toward your prospective partner. This person is about to become the center of your new life together. He or she deserves your respect and all your love.

WWW.LOVE

The following are Internet sites that feature love and compatibility tests and romantic ideas. Judge for yourself if they have any value. For the most part, they are useful for entertainment only.

www.queendom.com   Here you will find *many* tests, ranging from the jealousy to the relationship satisfaction test.

www.topchoice.com/~psyche/lovetest/   This website has developed a questionnaire that measures the dimensions of love. The scale is made up of sixty-eight items that describe love and are drawn from current research. It should take you under an hour to complete this love test and go through the results. You should take the test in private.

www.thelovecentre.com Take the self-quiz about love. It doesn't matter if you are single or have a mate. Take this test to discover your attitudes about love.

www.anglefire.com/ny/doctorl/ This site has many websites to help everybody on problems ranging from first dates to sex. If you're a little worried about talking about your relationship, you can take the relationship test. If your problems still aren't solved, you can e-mail the doctor.

www.rom101.com Discover discussion groups and comprehensive love tests. There are also dating ideas and games, romantic links, advice, and poetry.

www.lovecalculator.com Sometimes you'd like to know if a relationship with someone can work out. Therefore Doctor Love has designed this great machine for you. With the Love Calculator, you can estimate the probability of a successful relationship between two people.

www.marriage.about.com Here you'll find articles and discussion on anniversaries, communication, the